THE SAWDUST WAR

THE SAWDUST WAR

POEMS BY

Jim Barnes

UNIVERSITY OF ILLINOIS PRESS
Urbana and Chicago

Publication of this work was supported in part
by a grant from the Illinois Arts Council, a state agency.

This book is printed on acid-free paper.

Library of Congress Cataloging-in-Publication Data

Barnes, Jim
     The sawdust war : poems / by Jim Barnes.
         p.   cm.
     ISBN 0-252-06239-6 (pbk. : alk. paper)
     I. Title.
PS3552.A67395S38 1992
811'.54—dc20   91-27043
                                                           CIP

*"I have been stressed, and born, and stamped
Alive on this doorstep."*

       —James Dickey, "Doorstep, Lightning, Waif-Dreaming"

*"I learnt the verbs of will, and had my secret;
The code of night tapped on my tongue;
What had been one was many sounding minded."*

       —Dylan Thomas, "From Love's First Fever to Her Plague"

Acknowledgments

Grateful acknowledgment is made to the following publications in which many of the poems, some in radically different versions, first appeared:

The Berkeley Poetry Review: "In the Formal Garden" and "In Another Country"

Chelsea: "Crow's Firesticks" and "Crow White"

Chicago Review: "Postcard to James Welch in Missoula"

Focus Midwest: "Diving off the Bridge"

Greenfield Review: "Postcard to Brian Bedard from Somewhere on the Illinois, near Tahlequah, Oklahoma"

Helios: "Postcard to Alain-André Jourdier from the Longhorn Bar in Kirksville, Missouri"

Hellas: "At a Crossing, Somewhere in Ulster" and "For Roland, Presumed Taken"

High Plains Literary Review: "Fourche Maline Bottoms"

Interim: "Shaving the Dead"

Interstate: "Eulogy," under the title "They Still Dig Coal in McAlester, John Berryman"

The Journal: "Hogging below the Gates at Wister Dam"

Kansas Quarterly: "International Student Union Coffee Shop: Ramadan, after the Bomb Threat" and "Vesperal"

Kenyon Review: "After the Great Plains" and "Night Flight"

Memphis State Review: "The Planting"

The Nation: "The Sawdust War" and "Snowbound at the Bar 2, below Winding Stair Mountain, 1943"

Negative Capability: "Postcard to Mark Theriac from Taos, near Kit Carson's Grave"

New England Review: "The Ranch, Wild Horse Canyon, 1943"

New Letters: "You Know Who You Are: This Is for You, My Friend"

Nimrod: "Looking for an Epitaph"

North Dakota Quarterly: "The Poor Fox" and "Postcard to Terence Moser in Exile"

Paintbrush: "The Tower, 1945" and "Under the Tent"

The Phoenix: "Soliloquy in My Forty-seventh Year"

Poetry East: "After the Funeral," "The Cabin on Nanny Ridge," and "Near the Top"

Poetry Northwest: "Last Dream Song. A Fragment"

Poetry Wales: "Mali Chito"

Prairie Schooner: "Military Burial, Summerfield Cemetery: A Late Eulogy" and "Remembering Hiroshima and Propaganda"

Quarterly West: "Driving through Missouri"

St. Andrews Review: "The Garden"

Slackwater Review: "Drinking 3.2 at Mountain Top Tavern"

Tamaqua: "At the South Gate," "Castle Keep," "In the Melzi Gardens," "Mafia Wedding," "The Paying Stone," "Rowing over the Dead," "San Martino," "South Wind," and "Taking the Varenna Ferry"

TriQuarterly: "On Hearing the News That Hitler Was Dead"

Webster Review: "Wolf Watch: Winding Stair Mountain, 1923"

Wind: "Legacy of Bones," under the title "Legacy"

"Postcard to Kaz from Somewhere South of Allah" first appeared in *Circle of Motion: Arizona Anthology of Contemporary American Indian Literature,* ed. Kathleen Mullen Sands (Tempe: Arizona Historical Foundation, 1990).

At least one-third of this book would not have been written if it had not been for the generosity of the Rockefeller Foundation in awarding me a Bellagio Study Center Residency for five paradisal weeks in the spring of 1990. Never have I had such freedom to write and to enjoy the world. Villa Serbelloni will long remain for my wife and me what work and leisure should always be.

Contents

THE SAWDUST WAR

The Sawdust War

On the early summer days I lay with back
against the sawdust pile and felt the heat
of a thousand pines, oaks, elms, sycamores
flowing into my flesh, my nose alive
with that peculiar smell of death the trees
became. Odd to me then how the summer rain
made the heat even more intense. Digging
down the dust, I began to reshape a world
I hardly knew: the crumbly terrain became
theaters of the war. I was barely ten.

What I knew of the wide world and real war
came down the valley's road or flew over
the mountains I was caught between. Remote
I was nightly glued to the radio,
wondering at reports of a North African
campaign and Europe falling into chaos.
All daylight long I imitated what I
thought I heard, molding sawdust into hills,
roads, rivers, displacing troops of toys,
claiming ground by avalanche and mortar

fire, advancing bravely into black cities,
shrouding the fallen heroes with white bark.
I gained good ground against the Axis through
long summer days. Then one morning, dressed in
drab for hard work of war, I saw real smoke
rising from my battlefield. Crawling from
beneath the sawdust like vague spiderwebs,
claiming first the underground, then foxholes,

it spread like a wave of poison gas across
the woody hills I shaped with a mason's trowel.

I could not see the fire: it climbed from deep
within. No matter how I dug or shifted dust,
I could not find the source. My captured ground
nightly sank into itself. The gray smoke
hovered like owls under the slow stillness
of stars, until one night I woke to see,
at the center, a circle of smoldering sparks
turning to flame, ash spreading outward and down.
All night the pile glowed red, and I grew ashamed
for some fierce reason I could not then name.

Under the Tent

The traveling show stretched its canvas
over the bluegrass behind the store
when we were ten, the last picture
shows we'd get to see during the war

the Axis forced on us. We crouched
by the flapping tent. The summer wind
at night was mischief in our heads,
blowing wild thyme in our hair. Then

we were full of war, those of us
too young to go. We claimed to know
all battlegrounds through hell and back.
What we wanted to do was throw

enough of the dark upon our skins
to slip beneath all tents unseen,
as the night patrol did in the film
we saw that summer before the end.

We had to time it right: to roll
exactly under the tent the way
you roll away from quick danger
in your sleep. Or we'd have to play

the fool when the tentwalker caught
us by the neck. Our detailed plan
precise, we penetrated the held
blackness the exact moment when

the light went out and the silver
screen lit up, rolling in unison
into farmers' heavy legs, spittle,
sleeping dogs, climbing into sound

and light, an illumination
we understood more than the real.
Such ecstasy of risk carried us
into ourselves and into the world.

The Tower, 1945

Into the brush,
into the heart
of the thicket
we bored our way,
penknives held in
our hands or teeth.
We dragged in four
long, keen poles cut
from the ash grove
across the stream.
With braces cut
from smaller trees
we raised the poles
into the sky
lashing them tight
with inner bark
of elm trees. From
atop the tower
we could survey
all the world we
knew. In that clear
universe of
time, we held fate
in our hands and
warned far fields of
incoming flights
bent on bombing
all mankind. We
stood our ground as
formations flew
above the clouds

or Mustangs buzzed
the town a mile
off. When we swung
down with the sun,
to home and sleep,
the world went with
us, safe, free from
all risk until
at dawn when we
would wake again.

Near the Top

The wind rose early the day I climbed the oak
to carve my name on the trunk near the top,
where no one but me had been while Europe
burned. Daily I heard the war after dark
through the static of the battery radio.
Forever at home, I pressed myself into

the sky, up every kind of tree—white oak,
black gum, Chinese elm—as if the sun's rays
would give me wings to join the heavy race
of birds daily droning from dawn to dusk
across my limited world. All their dumb
luck wrapped tight about their bodies, they came,

tatooed and numbered on their silver under-
sides, planes skimming the tops of barns and trees,
taking in the wake waving arms of boys, leaves
falling heavy as flak. There was thunder
in the woods, in the homes of mothers of boys
then gone, and in the urgency of time—noise

of a world driven mad by a rush no wind
of history could ever understand. There
on the home front I gunned tops of trees. Barely
able to hang onto the trunk bending
from my weight, I carved my name into gray
bark and held fast as the top rolled and swayed,

not just from wind and weight but also from
Mustangs so close I felt the oily heat of
exhausts against my cheek, the roar above

all that I, soaring, had heard before. Numb
with the wild thrill of flight, that day I found
I had my war and rode the treetop down

through the tops of lesser trees to parachute
onto the alien earth that was my home.
My name would ride the sky filled with the drone
of planes. And I knew, when the night grew mute
with stars, part of me would still be up there,
loving the war, loving the dumbness of air.

The Cabin on Nanny Ridge

For days we felled the yellow pines
and shouldered them to the clearing we
had made at the rim of the ridge and swore
the way mountain men had done. Time
backed for us: we sang Cherokee
and Choctaw hymns, thatched the roof more

with words than limbs and needles from
the pines. We were innocent of all
that we surveyed. The world at war
was far enough away no bombs
that they told us fell could fall.
We lived without clock time, not sure

of the past we recreated or of
the squadrons daily overhead.
We lived the strategies we planned.
The days of summer when Europe
burned, we graved our dreamtime deeds
as runes below our small traced hands

on the stone north face of Nanny Ridge.
Forty years have grayed the glyphs,
and of the cabin nothing remains
but worms and a slow memory
of days we thought would never end—
before other wars changed our lives.

On Hearing the News That Hitler Was Dead

When we heard the news that Hitler was dead,
under the porch something shook we couldn't find.
The dogs were by our sides, and all the hogs
were penned. The radio was full of Europe's end
and Berlin falling into Red Russia's hands.

The grown-ups heard it and sent us in the house
with the dogs, their bristles tough as quills.
Something big bumped against the floor and made
the blackest sounds we'd ever heard. Then, still
scraping underneath, it roared aloud until

we turned as white as chalk and someone fired
a shotgun into the dark beneath the floor.
We heard hell break from down below and burst
through the front-yard picket fence: a panther
black as sin itself. They said it cleared a car

in one long leap and the ditch we couldn't jump.
We sighed and turned our normal brown as if
some threat of evil had missed us in the night.
The commentator's words on Hitler's death left
us puzzled about the course of war. A gift

of light was what we children waited for.
In the falling night we heard the far-off yowl
of wild cats in the woods, or thought we did.
The news leapt into the dark, wondering how
the master race so-called could master now

with Der Führer dead and the Russians drunk
on German schnapps. But what if he were not
the ashes they said were his? someone asked.
Silence and sound grew thick. Outside, lamplight
stumbled and fell into a starless night.

The Ranch, Wild Horse Canyon, 1943

The mountain south of the ranch leaned hard through
a heavy sky almost blocking the winter sun
at noon. The canyon ended there, dammed by the blue
haze that Winding Stair became after a winter rain
or snow. You could hear all the horses neigh at you

from the timbered slopes on clear December nights
when the wind was down. Stars were always on the move
across the narrow patch of sky. Lying just right
in your bunk by the window, you saw ridges shove
all the higher constellations across the night

and thought of all the things you'd like to do before
your light went out and your small voice was stilled. At ten
you were wise enough to want a few summers more
to ride the ranch with the hired hands, to pretend
no end of things. But things began to end. The roar

of warplanes overhead each day made the air dance
and the canyon echo with the drumming of stampede.
The rancher's elder son joined up, finding a chance
in war to leave for a wider world. You felt a need
to keep the horses free and cried to see them prance

into the boxcars, into soap and glue, to save
the world. Days were full of planes and nights of solemn
radio, commentators mournful and slow, wave after wave
of static as the battery wore down. You were dumb
with grief at the loss of horses, dumb with ways

to call them home, yet old enough to know the dead horses would not neigh again under the mountain moon. You wept as a child at the stockyard gate, your knees red with earth, and swore in time to come horses would run free as far as the mountain's end and the canyon's head.

Night Flight

The stillness of the coming night laid dusk
about the house, the yard, and the meadow
beyond. I felt something pushing the air
up from the river a mile away. The glow
in the west was dimming into stars and there

were quiet sounds of birds above the barn.
A larger shadow fell out of the north,
barely clearing the shivering tops of oaks,
opening the air with a gray rush to earth,
its feathered props fluttering, piston strokes

muted in the heavy air. And then the plane
was down and safe on stilted wheels. The time
it took me to run across the field was long
enough for the pilot to disappear. I climbed
upon a wing and counted rising suns

stenciled over the camouflaged cockpit
wall, the miniature flags a blood red.
The twin fuselages, dull as torpedoes,
absorbed the low moon. Prone, I laid my head
against the wing and heard ghost rockets go.

I could not fathom the plane's free-fall into
our meadow, no more than I could the tides
of the moon. Night grew still closer to the land,
the stars lighting the blades of grass like flares,
and the pilot returning to offer me his hand.

He did not say why he had landed there
so quietly, but waved me clear and made
the engines whine into their balanced lives,
gunning into the night but never to fade
from my memory of the war in 1945.

At a Crossing, Somewhere in Ulster

The ford at daybreak
ripples round
ogamed stones.

The horse stops
midstream,
looks down.

A faint noise of thunder:
somewhere on the river
a small fall.

Some wild bird condemning
our presence cries
upstream:

Cuchulainn,
a meandering chord,
Cuchulainn.

The horse regards
a pale reflection,
shifts his weight
and leather squeaks.

A finny perch
gulps past,
Cuchulainn,
measuring
a monody of loss.

Military Burial, Summerfield Cemetery:
A Late Eulogy

An honor guard brought the gray box down from
Tinker Field the day of burial. A few
of us came up the hill as if we knew
this man death and the flyers carried home.

How easy it is when you are nine or ten
to let your body go into the night,
into a dream of glory that's just right
for you. When you are nineteen and a man,

the dream is still a dream but need is there.
Nearly fifty years have gone since they lowered
him to this still place, his wings sculptured
granite now aloft in an angelic air.

I remember echoes in the woods: the sound
of taps soft in the late afternoon sun,
the stilling volley, the ceremony done.
Deranged by the time, I felt the trees around

the drab cemetery shudder in the light
wind rising in the clear south, and from
the west I heard a high plane's engines thrum.
Now it is hard to name what his last flight

was for: honor, glory, right, or just war.
Others have ended near him, on this hill,
from later skies. For all who had the will
for wings I have only words I wish were more.

25726350: Night, the Plain of Jars, and Dying

One last foot measures
the length of breath,
headed for the pinnacle
I call my chest.
Odd that he should drag
his slow foot up what
is Himavat to him.
Skirting the guts' red tide,
he plods along a muddy beach
careful not to be distracted
from the night's objective.
A single mucous track
must mark his way
from kneecap to
the uncertain valley
north of the rib cage.
He will come, this plodding
snail, his foot and mouth
tasting the brine of long-
forgotten seas, to heights
he gains when I am dead,
then drop off suddenly
to forget this mountain,
a one-shot night patrol.

Remembering Hiroshima and Propaganda

By night I was sure I would hear the blast.
I had waited all the day the radio
gave the news. Solemn as a sad Gabriel,
the spokesman for the White House hailed our flag,
our boys, and then the sheer force of our will.
The language was full of high hopes: at last

we could see an end to the war, all war,
they said. I listened hard for all of us
and heard little, as the sky filled with birds.
The radio droned on and on, and now and then
a plane, too high to see, drew me to the yard
where silence rode the air as never before

when the high thin sound was gone. After sundown
I listened for a distant drumroll, looked
hard for falling stars and a glow in the east.
Nothing struck me beyond my normal world.
I would not know the force of words unleashed
by bombing Hiroshima till the decades ground

my country more insane. I am not pleased
to stand on this cliff above the Pacific,
still listening hard for the end of time,
and hear those voices speak of how well we
have it now with cobalt skies and no crime
we can't track to its source with rays of peace.

For Roland, Presumed Taken

By the time we missed you dusk was settling in.
The first reaction was to think
of drowning, the deep hole just north of the house
that the spring flows into
out from under the sycamore.
You had played there earlier in the day
and had wanted to wade the still water
after minnows schooling the shadows.

We tracked you back to the spring, and I died
with fear that you would be floating
among the lilies, white as the ghost of fish.
But your tracks veered left
toward the valley where the cattle grazed,
then vanished in the flowing grass.
I blew the horn that called the cattle in.
You knew the sound and loved the way
the cattle came loping up at feeding time.

Roland, still, today, you cannot hear the sound of the horn,
cannot holler back up the mountainside
to let us know in your wee voice you are safe and found.
Why you walked off into the green of that day
we can never know, except the valley
and the mountain beyond must have yielded a sudden
sound or flash of light that took your eyes away.
And you were gone. It is as if

eagles swooped you up, leaving
not one trace to tell us the way you went away.
Nights I imagine the beat of drums,

the clanging of toy swords,
rocking horses neighing
on their tracks.
In another age
I would offer
up my glove
to God
to have you back.

Now, we have packed away your life
in boxes we store
in case the memory
we hold is swept away
by chance
or the slow years.

Snowbound at the Bar 2, below Winding Stair Mountain, 1943

It came from the southwest so fast it caught
us unawares, the wind whipping the autumn
snow across the road barely visible in
the early dark of evening, ten miles from
town and a lonely five from the valley homes.

I could hear the engine groan down the soft
road. My eyes squinted for Red Wing's barn roof
I knew should loom like a ship in fog around
the hairpin curve. For hours it seemed we crawled
along the mountain's side in a toy that hauled

ten times its weight, so heavy the bus in snow.
Then we saw the barn and stopped. The road
no longer passable, we the children
in great delight were herded across a wide
expanse of moonlit shadows, black on white.

They fed us black-eyed peas and sauerkraut,
and Red Wing played guitar and told us about
the wolves we heard howling outside the circle
of light the Bar 2 gave off. Hired hands brought
us blankets, spread them near the fire, their boots

heavy with the unexpected snow. Before
I drifted into sleep I heard the roar
of static on Red Wing's battery radio,
then Gabriel Heater's mournful voice full
of drudging war: no end in sight this fall.

Morning brought us back into a brighter world,
and long before the sun was high we hurled
ourselves into the rancher's white haystack,
pretending Bavarian Alps could never stop
such allies as we were from reaching the top.

Postcard to Kaz from Somewhere South of Allah

Dear Kaz, I miss the crosses by the roads
that made me slow before. They took them down
I guess to lure retirees home to Love
and other towns needing cash never seen
before. Hey, I crossed the Prescott range
at dusk to wonder if that steely sun
consumed the desert reservation north
of Blythe. Ho, the altitude allows wonders.
I know why Cochise fought. And Geronimo.
At Allah I had to rest the Mustang
and my head. All the way from Gallop I'd tried
to remember my tally of white crosses
for those who never made it. *Adios.*

Around the Cow Pond

Across the swale the blackbirds referee
something in the grass that I can't see.
Their war games make the cattails sway.

For twenty years I've watched them carry on
around the cow pond, their chevrons
sure signs of battle that are patched

onto the general genetic black.
These game birds do not fight for lack
of little to do, but for the rule

of grass where they lay borders neither cow
nor crow can safely pass without
a sound attack of black orders

only the dumb or dead would not obey.
There's something about those birds I say
will last as long as there is need

for birds and trilling cry of any sort.
Always around their reedy fort
they're ready with black word or song,

and whichever one I get depends on
what my mission is. Sticks and stones
or such are nearly as bad as guns,

but if I walk along with worms and pole
in hand, I know I'll hear them call
down battle flags and raise a song.

Skipping

Something never quite returns when you want
the facts the way you'd like the past to be.
It was our last day together: the sun
was bright, the new grass up, the water right,
and no one cared that we had missed the day.

You can't quite remember getting there, or
which of you did this or that: skipping stones
was in our blood. This was our vague good-bye,
a salute to the world of the narrow stream
we frolicked in and the school two miles away.

You never get it right without the weather:
the May sun warmed our cheeks. We swam till noon.
Then the girls spread lunch on the bank under
the sycamore tree. Above us the Tarzan swing
was a thread of the sun, and we drifted

on a wave of small thought and talk, already
forgetting what we had been those walled years.
But still it's not quite right: you remember
more than was. The love didn't really happen.
You were too shy, or the others were wrapped

up in future selves. You know that someone
almost drowned: two others pulled him out by
the hair. He'd dived too deep. There was a knot
on his crown. Or maybe he'd just faked it
for the tears the girls almost didn't shed.

What is this life? We should have asked stones,
grass, stream. We idled down the sun. The songs
we sang should have echoed off whatever
doom or dance we still beat time to. But they
fade, and the faces come up wrong, the facts

a reconstruction of no consequence. Once
you've done it, you never lose the knack of
skipping flat stones. How smooth the rock feels
against thumb and fingers as you release it
into its final spin and brief buoyancy.

Written during the Funeral of Hirohito

Earthbound they stood as monuments to air,
warplanes all rowed with their teeth to the wind
that thundered in from the lightning west. Mystery
covered them, black and drab hiding scars from
flak and cannon fire. Those beings from a sky
I did not know held me. Lights of the fair

flashed bare bulbs down the midway, and barkers
spieled sucker lines in megaphones. From my stance
beneath the tatooed nose of a Black Widow,
I saw the night slide over us, clouds and dim
stars inbound from the Pacific. In the far
hills west, a high roll of drums and faster

light. I remember rain, the splatter of large
drops on wings and tails, tents filled with air.
The planes off-limits, I snailed up a narrow
ladder propped against the cold cockpit
to lean heavenward on the clear canopy
of glass and feel the storm wind descend hard

to lift us off the world. All the world known
to me stretched off into the night below.
In a fantasy of war, I flew missions
no man could fly and returned shattered to do
again that which could not be done. I lived
in minutes a life I would not give the gone

years for. The tumult of the county fair rolled
under the night fighter's blackened wings. Held
clouds bursting into terrifying light,

the storm surrounded us. Parents ran for
cars, and children scampered through exhibits.
I was ten then and knew I had control.

Legacy of Bones

Children from another time
will shake their heads in disbelief
and cautiously brush the dust aside

when they have found at last our bones
upon the hill. And fear that passes
will pass for them upon the hill.

And guessing games that children play
will hold the hour of the day:
a monster hidden in a grove

attacked a lady here at night,
or a traveler from another world
stood lonely vigil here and died.

Our songs will grow dry in the wind
that passes through the mindless moon.
And we, the elders gone, will leave

our marks and knots and stones, but not
the words the children then will chant.
Drawing our bones upon their grids

with tools we never had, they may
pronounce us more than dust again.
For living language makes every-

thing happen, or nothing, as it rides
the tongue into desert places,
solitude where heart still resides.

AFTER THE GREAT PLAINS

After the Great Plains

Nothing remains the same in this long land.
Bird, fox, gully, grass, all are history
as soon as the moon rises or the wind climbs,
tales told by shadows leaning toward a vista
few eyes discern.

What strikes the windshield hardest as you drive
across is haze, distance claiming being
as absolute as the grasshoppers crushed on
the glass. There is no sameness to a land
that paints itself

different each dawn. The wind in your hair
today becomes a mouse's breath four states
beyond tomorrow. The river you ford could not
be any river. Particular, it flows through
the heart of the land.

After the Great Plains you are not the same.
No matter which way you cross something stays
firmly with you, a sense hard to name, like
a pebble in the toe of your boot you can't shake
out in this life.

Wolf Watch: Winding Stair Mountain, 1923

1. *Prelude*

Green turning yellow, the oaks
acknowledge first frosts, the days
browning into the slower season,
a paying time. The pines
alone hold their richer shades,
a greening that unchanging will
grow brittle in winter's winds.
Coveys of quails sun fat
beyond low limbs of blackjack
and huckleberry. Fawns have
lost their spots running into
a dream of endless buds. It
is a paying time, a time when
the gone months of summer
must be reckoned up. We know
it by the moon and the cries
down the canyon where the river
lies sure within its banks,
minnows schooling in shadows,
the shoals ringing with sounds
of the cattle's hoofs.

* * *

Beasts of timber, beasts of
mountain meadows. There
is no hope in this low
autumn sun. You know
killing time rides the wind.
Cries across the ridges

nightly come. The star hangs
red under Orion's belt.

2. *This is where I live*

Between Round Mountain
and Sycamore Tower, five
miles west of the military road,
ten miles southwest of Summerfield,
just here, is where I live.
The grass is good, rich in
the promise of mountain stone
unturned by horse and plow.
This is where I live.
Winters the cattle graze on
the fine brown native grass.
I am the last: other ranchers
have gone soft beyond
their fences. Here is where
I live: miles of timber,
hidden meadows stretch as far
as I can ride in a full
day's time.

* * *

I sing most days and sleep
well nights, until the first
frost comes and paying time.
I hold this place on earth
as mine and the Lord's.

But how to reckon with
the wolves keeps me
nightly on the go.
The herd gathers round
my cabin and lows me into
a sometime dream.
I try to keep them
calm winters when wolves
drag carcasses of calves
into their godless dens.

* * *

Wolf, wolf, I will
not stand as if before
a mirror and see you
tear my life out of
my hands. This is
where I live.

3. *The preacher*

You know, Brother, how you used
to ride home weekends. Service
ain't the same since you moved them
cattle farther south. Your testimonies
got the congregation going at tithing
time. The Lord knows you are his man.
But this here withdrawal into
the wilderness, I ain't sure
He sanctions it. I've talked

to him long about you and He
wants you home for Sunday services.
Baptizing this Sunday at the Gin Hole—
He'd like you to lead in prayer,
I know. I don't mean to scold,
but you know how it is: we've
got to keep the flock together.
I'll say so long for now. Sunday
we'll gather at the river sure.

4. *The beautiful, the beautiful, river*

If he thinks for a moment
I'll leave my herd for the sake
of a handful of doubtful souls,
dear Lord, he's loony and you
are no dream to believe in.
Some things matter more.
I'll take the cattle to the river,
all right, and they'll drink
their fill of clear, bright water,
and I'll sing, but not to
human ears and bent knees.

5. *Howl*

Wolf, listen to me, I have
a song to sing: if you drag
your scrawny hide within
gunshot of my domain,
I'll drop you'dead
as a junked doorknob.

      * * *

Howl, howl, and damn your pride.
When I swore to cherish God's creatures all,
I lied, innocent as hell in the Sunday heat.

6. *For company's sake*

Evil things, the stories go.
I like them, cantankerous
and fussy, murderous
as old maids. Black
as an ace of spades and crooked,
they'll steal you blind
if you get too friendly.
You learn to talk crow
here for company's sake.

      * * *

A herd of cattle,
a flock of sheep,
a school of fish,
a covey of quails,
a murder of crows,
a pack of wolves.

7. *The wife*

When he left it was for summer grazing.
Well, I know him now as I never did:
he loves his cows more than God and me,
and that's a shame. All these years
we've never butchered beef. The marriage,
yes. Of this debt, mark it paid in full,
O Lord. All men are sonsabitches.
This has got to end. Neighbors talk behind
my back. I have no friends. My hands
are cold nights and dreams trouble me no
end. Not much now, dear Lord, on this earth
for left women and children grown and gone.
My days are full of the dark of weeds:
the hoe strikes jimson and cocklebur
to no avail. Nothing fruitful grows
in this garden. Fall and neglect
come early this season. *Fall:*
get sick: something: come home: Amen.

8. *The name*

All night I've lain here thinking
what it is I must have forgotten.
Something has gone out of the day.
The wolves are preying on the herd:
two calves missing now and the lowing
drones in my ears. That's not it.
What I have done with my life
I'd do again. I've known men who've
had passion for the hunt, those who've
chased women crazy all their days.
I've known them plenty. I don't know
where I stand, except this is the life.
I tally up the days, and always
something beyond the herd is missing.
I cannot name its name. There's
a sound collecting in the wind
I know and do not know.

9. *The watch*

We found him beneath a willow,
miles from the herd, on the bank
of Cedar Creek, at rest, his back
against the grooved trunk, eyes open
and sighting down the sun, his horse
hobbled two mountains over at
the cabin. Eyes straight and fixed west
on the sun, he held a space

beneath the tree with what the preacher
called a fierce determination.
Tracks of wolves lined the bank,
at least a dozen different
but no human sign, not his own.
Why here was the question asked.
The heart had stopped—
and nothing else. We carried him
horseback through the coming night.
Ridges away the descending
yap and yowl of wolves
were death song for
the last of a breed.

10. *What waits*

Under the quiet trees the wolves are blankets of fur.
The half moon strikes her faint light on first snow,
and there are stars that seem as white as candle flame.
The low of a ruminating herd sounds the dark.
A river of night runs smoothly through the soft land.
All things abide awhile in time.
What waits, poised for spring, walks in cadence with the night.

Driving through Missouri

"That is no country for old men."
— W. B. Yeats

Missouri. Mid-autumn is as still as ice.
The dust lies as pale as moonlight twice

shone. Everywhere, the evidence of drought
and a certain dying still to come. Without

the gold of harvest moon to bring this night
down monuments of clouds and shadows right

for song, what good the gold mosaic of
a word? I gather all my light love

into an artifice of now, see a snow
drifting at the bottom of my eye, although

I am contending with the real, the road.
I'd like to clap my hands and sing the woods

rich in rainy, salmon leaves and new light,
set a course for stars deep in a softer night,

a night I could make a song on. Out of
this pale time there's still a thing or two to love.

Postcard to Alain-André Jourdier from the Longhorn Bar in Kirksville, Missouri

Cher ami, this bar's name is too far west
for cornfields streaming toward hybrid Iowa.
There's not one Flathead or one Sioux. Or one
song that's worth crying over. You've gone east
looking for your name and a chance to write
the truth. I'm stuck to corn and students who
have never learned to talk to ears and pray.
I'm doing contemporary American poetry now.
I drink too much, and read Merwin and Jones
with a stutter. Levertov's wrinkled cunt poem
falls cave-dark and flat. As usual, the window
holds the day as rain beats down. There is no
hope now, mon ami: through the glass I see
a fierce wind growing in the west, dark in
desperate towns where other lives go wrong,
a wind we have to ride. A dark day, my friend,
but after this wild rain, I'll set my mind
dancing to the sun and write you lighter things.
I'll say: there's something in the air, Indians
and songs are coming back to stay. *Au revoir.*

The Poor Fox

The hounds of autumn have bayed the poor fox
    in a cave that bats keep
and the rider races on, siccing, yelling,
    coming on at full gallop,
the red coat flashing, the brass horn banging
    against boot and stirrup,
and the hounds of autumn begin a circling dance
    with tongues and paws
expecting fur, though none expected the poor fox
    in the bats' cave to pause
and grin at the sound of spurs, at the sound
    of song, then dig deep,
deep down to the primeval womb of warmth
    where he might sleep or doze,
while the determined hounds trumpet and trail
    and claw through the maze,
until that space in time that he chooses guile
    again to lead him back up
from the labyrinth of bats' bones to the mouth
    of light where he might jump
and career across green fields, roads, rivers,
    and in his own way weep.

Fourche Maline Bottoms

Kid, they told me, those raucous neighbor boys,
you won't find nothing down in them bottoms
worth a shit. I showed them nothing but thumbs
and fingers waving ears. I knew what poise
to take and still avoid their wrath. The joy
of finding arrowheads beneath the crumb-
ling leaves was something I could never come
to trade for any neighbor's game. No toy
could ever do what flint or milky chert
could do for my own small mauled imagination.
For seven years I sifted coal-black dirt,
found arrowheads so keen I knew I'd seen
into my own ancestral past where hurt
and harm stood taller than neighbor boys had been.

Postcard to Brian Bedard from Somewhere on the Illinois, near Tahlequah, Oklahoma

Dear Brian, you wouldn't think these cliffs hold bones
that knew the earth was mother and the river below
food for more than thought. Burials abound
that put most mummies to real shame. The skin
is too tight across the teeth, though, to sing
again of white-water runs and black bass,
the ears too cracked to catch the sound of solemn
wind, the echoes of ghost arrows ricocheting
cliff to cliff. It's too bad, Brian, we lift them up
from a lap they knew from birth, from a dignity
so deep we can learn only they knew how
to die. I've looked for the bear we heard about
roaming these woods. The closest I've come is
a birch scored a hundred years ago or more.

The Planting

Beside the ash bending
in homage to summer wind,
I will plant the elm, rooted
in the earthen bowl you turned.

The blood-red moon, rising,
will witness my druid's hands,
and what I speak in the night
over grass and stone will long

hold these limbs and roots
together as we have sworn
our love till death. Not from seeds
are these two to live, but from

a felt bond, a breath,
I now make as we ourselves
made promising till death.
And while trees stand, not just

these two, but all, so too we—
within soft hands of each other,
yet free in the summer wind
to rise and fall, touch or not touch—

will stand straight in love's gravity.

The Garden

for Leo Van Scyoc

Behind the professor's house, the path runs down the hill into the woods, snakes through half an acre jungle, climbs into a hidden clearing. A garden: a few last tomatoes, grapes, squash, a row of dill. *Nel mezzo del cammin di nostra vita mi ritrovai* the nude scarecrow's headband reads, disappears into a ragged skull. On touch he dances. His privates flop. A crow laughs back in shadows, *I'm old and wise.* The professor doesn't mind. He knows his garden like a book. There's Eve's last leaf, for example, she left behind. Indian summer. Frost soon. He picks a tick, finds another, mutters, scratches his crotch. The melons didn't make a bulb. More manure. Keen in thought he sits at the foot of the crab apple tree, crumbles a lump of dirt from the garden he'd raised this year.

Crow White

You know how crow got black, don't you? Well, it was like this. Once he was white, really white, and a master of birds and men. You know, he felt sorry for the people. They got cold in the winter. They had to eat raw fish. So crow decided to discover fire. He went to the mountain where the thunder lived. No fire. He went to the valley where the rainbow lived. No fire. I'm stupid, he said. Why didn't I think of that before? I'll go to the sun, he said. Oh, the people said, oh. I'm going, he said. And he did. Then something terrible happened. The sun must have got mad. The sky was filled with fire everywhere and burnt snowflakes drifted down. The people said, it's a miracle, that black snow. They prayed to the sun. Then they heard something. It was very weak. Caw, it said, caw. They looked over behind a bush, which had begun to burn. They were afraid. But it was only crow. He was very weak and very black. It was some tough fight, he said, but I won.

Crow's Firesticks

The people didn't know how to work the firesticks. So they threw them into the ocean. A whale swallowed the sticks because he liked the way the sticks bent in the water. Crow was looking for the sticks on the beach. He was feeling better now, a little tired, but all right. He just wished they hadn't thrown those sticks away. He saw the whale with smoke coming out of the air hole. Crow flew out and went down the air hole. But when he got inside, the whale shut the trapdoor and it wouldn't open. Crow got real mad. But he couldn't get out. So he decided to cook some supper with his firesticks, which were there in the whale's belly. Crow liked blubber better than grubs. He made a big fire and whacked off a big piece of blubber. It got hotter and hotter in the whale's belly and crow started coughing and calling help, help, help. Some people in a boat speared the whale and cut open the belly and let crow out with his firesticks. Phew, he said, phew, that was close.

Postcard to Mark Theriac from Taos, near Kit Carson's Grave

Dear Mark, the wind stinks of sin you can't define,
some savage deed done for sake of code or lust.
The wind from the south is always hot, the Tewas
say, the growing season much in need of rain.
This is hardly Carson's land: you can't hide rot
from wind. We came to find ourselves outside
ourselves. What we find is obscured by cottonwood
snows and Spaniards slightly out of tune and race,
though at one rare place we saw a bear wash
his dish with red sand, and at the Kachina Lodge:
rows of painted root dolls and Tewas dance for rain
their eyes told us they didn't really want to come.
My son thinks Kit was Walt Disney's horse. Carolyn
says don't explain. This Sunday shows the Spaniards
still know their locks and crows are pecking fetishes
in red dust. More to come after rain. *Paix.*

Drinking 3.2 at Mountain Top Tavern

This bar has always been somebody's home
away from home, a place a man could tell
a lie and laugh. Or drink himself into
a sky wide as prairies he'd like to ride.
Used to be, I should've said. The owner's dead.
Likewise the lie and laugh. The beer reeks warm.
No dancing. No gambling on pool. No loving.

The sky cuts cold against the cracking panes.
One door, shattered above the knob, is wedged
tight by a rusty army knife. A half-breed
Choctaw hums to his hungry heart. He wants
his blood to feel fast the black and silver
hanging at his waist, the wings upon his boots.
We keep our strangers' talk out of his song.

The sun's half down, and there are vultures
in the sky a man has yet to count before
the sliding shadows cross his eyes and fade.
The half-breed knows, and takes his leave before
his closing note, before the silence drives
him deaf. Black against the approaching night,
he lifts his fist hard against the setting sun.

Mali Chito

The western rim hunched
under the black weight
pressing down like wet slack
in a burnt-out forge smoldering.
Not a thing stirred in that
blank sunset: whippoorwill,
snake, owl, coyote, man,
woman. Silence held uneasy
dominion. Then from the low
southwest came the roar
of a thousand furnaces
closer and closer until
all at once it dropped
in the hammering twilight,
gyring down a typhonic
bellows spewing pure
power and smelling of
Mexico and sagebrush,
barn roof and torn trees,
rose petals and human fear.

Postcard to James Welch in Missoula

Dear Jim, I am writing you today because
the sky is wrong and the bass won't bite
when the sign is in the groin. I've driven
300 miles through Missouri: everywhere rivers
and corn are coated with the dust of your
rain gone wrong. When I said dance, damn it all,
I meant make it work. Isn't it odd how
we think we have the old pump handle
in hand, then find our grip's empty air?
Remember when you were here, how the sky
was right with clouds and the wind scalped
us down to skull. You told us in a glance
the moving days are best, when sounds strike
the inner ear from places only the hawk
can name and some wild damned Indian,
eyes full of rainbows and fast jacks. *Achukma!*

Hogging below the Gates at Wister Dam

In spring flood time the Corps of Engineers
opened the gates to let the water level
down, and the exiled bass, bream, catfish, drum,
rushed the sluice in such numbers you could feel
them brush your legs. I came at night to wade
the rapids, hogging any fish I caught
into gunnysacks. I was too crazy
for fish to let them pass upstream to their
lost homes and rut among the dark drowned leaves.

What mattered then was innocence and guilt,
of which the fish knew nothing. I watched
old men daily take their limit of bass
or bluegill or channel cat. I knew it
was wrong in the game warden's eyes to hog
when only one hook per line was allowed.
I knew it was wrong the old men took fish
for the sake of eggs alone. I forgot moral
things as the sun went down and the moon said go.

What matters now is much the same, except
the fish are gone, have been gone these forty
years, the cycle cut by dam and hogging boys
and old men mad for the taste of fresh fish eggs.
Now you can wade the Poteau anywhere
below the dam and never feel a fin
or scales brush your legs. Few fish are drifting
here. The water is docile even in flood,
and the moon has no voice, and the fish no home.

ELEGIES FOR JOHN BERRYMAN
AND OTHERS

Elegies for John Berryman

1. *Diving off the Bridge*

Going off
the top
is like
all acts
I shall
never do
& breaking
through is
like oh
my god
why hast
thou &
it is
dark down
& cold
where mud
hangs on
but going
back up
the world
is real.

2. *Eulogy*

Never knew you till you died.
Shame on me. Pittsburg County
coal kept me black
& pure.

Didn't know a poet could be born
in such a dirty town
noted only for cheap coal
& Italians who cooked
cats in their spaghetti.

Till you died. Never knew you
cursed my native ground. Fuck
you, you said, & meant it
the way you meant it
long before you grew a beard.

They still dig coal in McAlester,
John Berryman, & black-assed
miners know a poet's
sacred meat.

They all knew your old man
but thought you died in battle
a long time ago.

3. *Looking for an Epitaph*

"Il sut aimer."
—*Guillaume Apollinaire*

Well, John. I'm thinking of you today & how
you knew to love your life in spite of father
mother friends yourself.
Holy Hell. You jumped the gun & left us
on a day it rained real pitchforks
in Minnesota.

Henry & friend came back. Why not you? Risk it,
with a stratagem, digging up like mad. Be
mad, it helps. Let us believe
Dante hot & political, full seven
circles down & raving Rome, Ravenna, etc.
plucked your beard.

—Mr. Bones, I's back & black as any Smith.
Sinned again. Par'n me, please. I won't stop cause
you done did yourself.
Weather's fine. Your Muse want to know where you
is. Screw him, she says, & I says: good god,
you did.

4. *Last Dream Song. A Fragment*

The policeman waved like trying to stay hail.
Henry waved, replied
with a nosedive into the concrete current
cutting beneath the bridge.

—Mr. Bones, you done done it now.
You is de dead end
we sweep up dat swept down.

You were a gone bird for de policeman's
scaredy-cat eyes. What you thought
when you said hi-dee-do wid dat wave
& took off off your perch
you'll never tell.

We don't mourn, Mr. Bones. We moan.
We knows de truth.
You done made a mess of thangs.

Le Louvre

Walking the Tuileries' gravel way
in the early summer, we see
the vista open into art
above the Seine.

The old masters are always home,
never hiding in corners or
faking it with modern faces,
but watching doors.

They greet us with a famous smile
or seem to take us by the hand
as if expecting us to come
to them again.

And now and then a brace or more
will throw some light on what our lives
have dimmed and sweep all love into
our arms alive.

Beyond the walls the traffic flow
beside the Seine and the poplars
is fierce with worldly attitude
and fumes. Drivers

seem bent on passing by this maze
of afterlife that finally leads
us gently home to contemplate
our lesser deeds.

We write our friends in St. Louis
on cards bought from the concierge,
Reubens' *L'Apothéose du Roi:*
wish you were here.

You Know Who You Are: This Is for You, My Friend

You went west to where mountains stop,
and did not stop but built a home,
a whole new life that was not new
to you but real as Kansas loam.

Always in your mind was that far
place whence you came and that far place
where you were. Distance you would bridge—
root, trunk, limb—all the ways

you could say *Friend* and mean it such
a way no stream could be denied.
The door stands open in that home,
the special chair for us reserved.

Friend, take this small token, if you
will, as tribute from all of us
who have too long remained silent
about your heart and human trust.

Shaving the Dead

1. *Djuna*

The Barnes sawed nightwood while drunk and bored
en Paris. All the worms left in, and T. S.
thought it Elizabethan and—tsh, tsh—
tragic to no end. Lord, the language soared:
those birds lodged in their floundering feathers
dusted despair, their wrong hopes braided into
eyebrows dark above monocles and soup.
Eggs eaten and eggs dropped confound whethers

and wherefores all this is worth it. So why
not dogs? She stood, stands, arrived in rank
unrighteousness. The dour humanity
doth not shine. It shows, she says, so there.
The loony night turns its gray belly up, and wood
fallen fails and the weird menagerie of care.

2. *High Fashion*

Onward O'Connor *et al.* Ireland's green
fromage. Saints bark back Joycean. I sing
Suzanna. Way back a tree falls, a string
breaks, and a wilderness begins to creep
toward Armageddon to be shorn, worn
over the scars of Jews. You think I know?
Don't ask me who made these crowns of thorn
fashionable. Dior perhaps. He's got dough.

Welcome, fools. It's the night before All Saints'.
So beggars must be bright and make believe
death's right to beat his drum *te deum te deum.*
Pass the chocolates and let's dance, old churl.
It's Lord have mercy, beauty, you are here at last.
I love your beasty toes, goddamn my soul, I do.

3. *Mexcali Blues,*

Old Malc carried his tattered book abroad
and into every Sussex pub and said: it's me,
see, this thing I did, it grew, it's me
just. Whoever believes that odd fellow out, nod
and wink. They drank around his slipping gut,
not near. He dreamed wrong Oaxaca and ginned
until all the fame flowed past his nose, pinned
neatly to the rocking floor where lay God

grinning in a shroud as loud as Turin,
right where old Malcolm always knew He was.
Page one hundred eighty-three gouged his eye.
He blurred on labors twelve but couldn't turn
crucified. English dogs pariahed and spiders rose
through cracks in tile. His misadventure would not die.

4. *or Death by Misadventure*

He'd see to that, and so that night he died.
Pilgrims, take your staff in hand, bread and wine.
Let's be off. We have a sing to say, a line
we'll try on whatever hot god he tried.
Let's see: there's Jehovah, but he's gone lame.
It's a long way to Sussex cemetery.
We'll count druids, then throw stones at *Lowry*
to wake that smoking god and ask what's sane.

You understand: we don't believe that sin's
a personal thing. From a long line of bad sonnets
we all proceed, and read the garden signs.
In Oaxaca, death is a daily count.
We'll take that drink to damned old Tezcatlipoca
and toasting hear *him* preach the mirror on the mount.

5. 666

They cried, died, when all the low blows landed
cancerous and slow. The dark wounds bled, bled,
and the High Ones passed through circuits in the head;
presses rolled, critics spat, and books were branded
great or classic because They are not here.
Hardly reason enough my reason says,
but who am I to say where illusion lies?
Let them have it while mayflies buzz and tear

brief wings. I'll hold the masters to my heart
for a stethoscopic view. Bell tower bright
on a sunlit day, the assassin knows his part.
Who's who is hard to tell from many a height.
Hot Texas lauds Whitman (Martin Sheen!) in his tower,
but spurns dear Sylvia in her hot metallic bower.

6. Doxology

Lord, love a duck! I can't get over you!
The same sad song comes hillbilly, speakers
blaring as odorous as dung. I chew
Hank's words romantic to keep the snickers
back, and pretend I'm living a heavy Mann,
mountainous under unseasonable August snow.
Other scholars go after Frost, not to know
the work. Such affective fallacies we can

dismiss as tripe, but not the life within
the work, the reeling world made whole again,
and there's the rub that makes the writer right.
World ever shall be and world without an end
if read again. What's classic to a state of mind
is what lasts long in mind, what long outlasts the night.

7. *Pussycat*

There's Berryman, the hurry man; he bridged
it to the end. Some swell jump that, or dive,
he did with one last wave to the bulging eye
of the law below. Yeah, Henry waved and hitched
up his baggy pants going down. White folks
don't cotton to Old Bones's being all black
and call him a schizophrenic pimpled hack
eben in heben where he sits and chokes

back them moans and groans he always didn't make.
All for you (and them), Old Bones, this whole show.
You damn well odysseyed all right, epic
to your scrawny toes. So bow for one last take,
Old Pussycat. With you away the mice will—Oh,
you have left us with puzzles harder than Beckett's.

8. More Advice to the Critics

Let's not forget old Hem. He snuffed it out
like his pop and yours, J. B. I need the myth,
the tall tales, the macho real-world beard with
no phoney dime-store tint. His short, stout
prose sustains, and Africa remains black
and whole. I'll'never see him other than
among green hills and watering holes. Man,
he snuffed it out in Idaho. No back-

ing up. Earth's the proper place for Papa,
and he will grow beyond the valley where
women's rights bad-mouth him now. Amended
he will never be: he clipped himself. There's no
shaving the dead when head is work and work is head.
Donc, zut alors! honi soit qui mal y pense.

International Student Union Coffee Shop:
Ramadan, after the Bomb Threat

A bad record scars the day
like a scimitar dragging in sand.
The grainy echoes hang for hours,
a monotony in glass.

The violated booths still invite,
though the last bazaar has fallen out of time.

The light's a poor oasis:
neither verse nor wine nor bold belch
breaks the Bedouin air.
The melon gaze
of dancing girl is gone.

Only the music
holds the sundown
as night falls
like an ill-stretched tent
in this place
of easy disguises and coffee dreams.

Looking for Le Bosquet, Oklahoma

Beneath the mountain's stone
black earth holds this heavy dusk.
All the graves are lost, epitaphs
written on brittle grass,
no survivor left to keen.

Only the moan of wind through pine
can find and name again
Le Bosquet town. The earth
lies broken, the shafts beneath
the hill hollow as ancient tombs.

Below the hill, where the mine breaks
from stone, a lone hawk plots for game
those acres that hide odd names
and eyes not even hawks want to see.
Le Bosquet's past is black

with ghosts and cinders night
is heir to and the screes.
Cries of a nightbird settle
on the land: distant the call
of dead Basques for the Pyrenees.

Postcard to Terence Moser in Exile

Dear Terry, there's a droning in the blood
tonight like some latter-day Kiowa cruising
up the Yellowstone looking for tribal stones
his forebears hid. Inside the arteries
there are caravans on roads that all head
west: they roll through countries tame as velvet,
wild as rawhide chewed soft by old squaws' gums.
On the wrong side of the continent, you too
must feel your blood take roads and make insane
treks to mountains where stones are real. Surreal
cycles of the blood pulse me through valleys we
know, but I'm miles away from my father's land.
The gears are worn, but hope's high. Keep the faith.

Vesperal

After invading fields
for grain, grasshoppers,
cornworms, cockroaches,
a long cloud of purple grackles
streams southward—I've seen
it last hours—overhead.
Sundowns I semaphore
from my front steps, one hat
in hand, a hat on my head,
waving a mad arm,
as if to warn
some coasting ship
of imminent rocky peril.
The neighbors think I'm mad,
lost in a sincere senility.
They don't know I love
those bombastic birds—
but crap blasting onto
my drive, roof, house-side,
windows, patio, deck,
bikes, car, dog, wife even
is more than enough to move
me toward a wild salute
those aviators understand.

Soliloquy in My Forty-seventh Year

Frost in owl light and first spring signs
dot the black tops of elms brown,
a budding slight but fierce, insistent
on turning day
to milder time:
the latest death of winter brushes the down
of the nested young, the cry of becoming, this
limbed brood, this open-throated prey

of the hovering hawk. Time is ever on,
and into my forty-seventh year, I lunge,
having leapt the younger ages in a blind
blink the owl's
eyes make in
their staring, blood-speared, no-heart vision
of utter uncontrollable innocence behind
the hill barn, above the numb morning fowls.

The house, low by the river, chimes with pan
bells, a prelude to breakfast and rising wind,
my goodwife always tunes
the times I die
into my torn
duds, staggering toward duties in yard,
and field above the yard, where cow flops bloom
and will bloom egg, worm, and the maggot's fly.

I shall not walk softly to atone,
nor in anger move my own, but shall kneel
now on this bare side of hill
and kiss the dust

and touch the stone
leavings of dropped stars, turds, the spiel
of spider and grass, and sing clear and swill
the late life come dumb into my trust.

After the Funeral

In memory of Bessie Vernon Adams Barnes

After the funeral come low wind and rain,
teared chatter of cousins, slow coughing cars,
sons and daughters edged with anxiety,
clods pounding the casket as spades erupt.
Somewhere near, back of it all, the lost boy
nods a last farewell, remembering roads,
departures, behind a grown man's gone eyes.
The moaning wind shakes the trees, and hair
flies free beneath the veils of wilted kin.
She would not have me standing in winter's
holy rain to stay her light soul, nor wish
to be other than gently dead when the walls
of death are down. I stand puddled and partial
in the deathwind of wonder, not wholly here,
but there on a high hill holding her hand
in a child's fear that she would sometime let
go and I would slip into the darkness
that is not sleep and not awaken to her
early morning sounds at the kitchen stove.
Still, I alone am Bessie's bard. Long let
stand her stone by the clod-cleaved cavity.
I cannot mourn but to whisper wet words
she would find foreign to her thick tongue,
scarce as her own words were, thin and seared
from use. No more than a handful sufficed her
all the crippled days she scrubbed the crooked
houses fresh as frost. She would thinly chide
me for these words, and her thin lips would break
into a blessing smile, and I would know

in our Welsh dumbness runs a blood that's thick
enough to last. I will hammer a slab
of words to honor silence and the wind
as Dylan did for bent Ann. I will chisel
a mother's life broken by tiles and stairs,
by early tumors twisted in her guts,
by waiting for the late knock of death.
Worm-blind and lost, I will grave the low words
into a song for her—and for the wind
that never stops for a mundane circumstance.

IN ANOTHER COUNTRY

Castello di Vezio, above Varenna

Our knees and hip joints breaking
into shards with every groaning
step upward,
we take

the humid late spring air into
our lungs, panting heavily through
mouths as dry
as sand.

Leaning hard into the first hill,
we climb into our breath and kill
our hobbled
legs more

on moraine pebbles underfoot,
mortared into the mountain roots,
than from grade
or altitude.

As the path narrows through high grass,
there is suddenly a stone house
and another,
a village

that we never saw from across
the lake. We expected thick moss
and castle walls
and olives,

not a town behind the tower
nor the echoing bells counting out our
ascent for
miles around.

But this is Lombardy, skies
of people everywhere, their eyes
peering out of
cars, trains,

out of garlic gardens, villas
of fragrance so rich, so full of
centuries, we
want to trust

the Alps. The door in the castle
wall is thick enough to last till
some other kingdom
comes to hold

this view. We cannot see forever
through the haze, but still far enough
to know we too
must go down.

Above Bellagio, Looking North to Varenna

Below the wall gulls circle mewing like Siamese cats,
their red eyes nearly visible against the black
water three hundred feet straight down. The wall you sit
on has crumbled for two thousand years of white gulls
and alternating heavy winds from north and south.
Two miles away, west in Tremezzo, they shot
Il Duce before the partisans trucked him south
like beef to hang upside down in Milano. Postcards
never show the land behind the landscape. Rocks drop
daily. Boats skirt the cliff where graves slid down into

the lake. No tourist ever asks about the war
and the days worth remembering. Here none forget.
Ask anyone. Back home we know nothing: words we
ought to stencil across our backs before we come
to hydrofoil Lake Como and pillage clothing stores.
Varenna glows under red tile in the warm May sun,
and the spying Castello di Vezio grays over
the town. The sound of bells you can't locate until
the late ferry leaving Bellagio blasts its fog
horn toward Menaggio. All sounds seem funneled up

the promontory as if the ruins were taking notes
for some long work on the history of foolish lives.
Say it would read like this: we came to Lombardy
for the sake of health. Or better: we came here wanting
nothing and found our eyes. You can see the snow of
Switzerland to the north, the waves reflecting Alps
in their white caps. The wind is southerly today.
Rain is a sure thing, perhaps the only thing that

is, between here and Varenna. Mussolini
gambled and lost, the Swiss border an hour away

but still too far. Little wonder why he ran: he
forgot the little guy, the Nazis, and the Alps.
The lines in stone are older than this light. You can
feel a stronger sun in the flint than the Villa
Serbelloni snails have known. Too many ends of things
on this hill: Pliny's villa god knows where, the dog
the princess loved, maybe even Dante's ghost up
from Limbo as guide. No cantos are large enough
to hold the spirit of this place. The water is deep,
and the Alps lean hard into Lombardy's shifting winds.

The Boats at Pescallo

Waiting out the long south wind
the boats rock with waves
swelling in

from miles beyond Villa Giulia.
Every afternoon the boats ride
high on their moorings. All July

they will be free
to take the force of inland squalls
and head for Villa Melzi

in full regatta. So sad
now these boats, whose
masters have had

to leave them for silk
works in Milano:
they sway like

dancers to slow violins.
But soon, their sails unfurled,
they will cut through winds

carrying a thousand years of ghosts
around the promontory
and the cliffs

of Serbelloni. The boats roll
in the deep bay.
A blackbird calls

melodious as a choral song.
On the hill the wind is in the olives,
and the Frati is red under the midday sun.

In Another Country: A Suite for the Villa Serbelloni

In memoriam Roberto Celli

* * *

1. *May 1990, Tremezzo, Where Mussolini Died*

"Villa Carlotta where Mussolini died,"
your tour guide speaks, among the roses and bells,
to a Nippon history buff whose Nikon levels
on the villa's azaleas on each side

of the brilliant terraces. Il Duce lied
to them in Rome and ran for the villa
and fascist friends, ran to merchants in silk,
lords who promised him Switzerland. You fight

the urge to strangle the guide and make him get
facts right. Tremezzo two hundred yards away
shuts down for lunch. The long Italian noon

blanches stone walls where yesterday you met
his ghost arm in arm with Sophia Loren's gray
sister, Claire, who, with her slender free hand,

carefully held her dress down against the wind,
against the dance of dust where all love ends.

2. *Francesca e Paolo: Bellagio*

A jewelry store with everything my wife
imagines golden about Lombardy. Of course,
we go in, past cheap coral and a horse
on a plastic pedestal. The lovely life

of Dante's airborne sinful lovers lifts
our eyes, lusty flesh tones some painter forced
out of black velvet. All the junk we swore
we would avoid draws us in as if

we have no will against the dime-store lures
glittering under glass. Outside, the ferry
sounds its horn, and Charon draws the gangplank

in, the passengers for Tremezzo sure
they will reach Villa Carlotta. I say
we are just looking, and feel my Italian sink

as the pale proprietress insists we hold
the bookmark she tells us is pure spun gold.

3. *Mule Track to Suira*

Last days in Bellagio and we want to walk
the cobbled paths the Lombards call mule tracks.
For us, hard trails. From Pescallo we take
the walled trails and groan upward. We can't talk:

Lake Como air is lead and fog. The chalky
walls sweat, and the green vineyards beyond sag
with blooms. At Villa Belmonte we shake
the sweat from our hair, panting and balking

at the steep climb for the sake of climb we set
ourselves upon. Above the fog the track
levels out. We walk easily along the crest

down through Aureggio, the smell of bread
surrounding us and the sun upon our backs,
then turn upward again, toward Suira, past

a hill garden and an old woman who waves
at us for love of garlic or strange faces.

4. *To Loppia*

Leaving Suira and the hard climb from Villa
Giulia's broad allee that cuts across
to Loppia as level as the lake, we are lost
in a maze of walled trails and the tropical

plants that cannot be there but are: the hill
is home to a forest thick with Spanish moss
and palms. We gauge the stone trail by fossils
too strange for this world and find it is still

the same hard road it has always been. The red
roofs of Loppia come into view. The long
lake boats, like a gypsy caravan at a fair,

are decked with silk from Como or fish, lead
sinkers and nets hanging from their prows. A song,
oddly Streisand, hangs on the morning air,

and we know this too is Lombardy, where
the bells can ring familiar at any hour.

5. In the Melzi Gardens

On the shore of Lake Como, looking westward,
Dante leans toward his Beatrice. In white
stone they are frozen in the midst of bright
azaleas. The warm spring sun has lured

us down from the Villa Serbelloni, the lords
of discipline having left us late last night.
How hard it is to write, even though you might
enjoy a fellowship, with the ghosts of bored

artists hovering about this pavilion.
We would like to reach the absolute in art,
the meaning behind the flowers and the stones,

a labyrinth that nearly takes our own
concept of paradise away with the riot
of rhododendrons and Dante's face grown

soft with love. Here in the Melzi Gardens
we look for light that will let our words go on.

6. *San Martino*

San Martino shines like a pocket of cinnabar
under the warm noonday sun. The trail up
always seems hard, the church perched on a lip
of gray stone that threatens to tumble over

the terraced gardens. There is always more
we can do easier than make that trip:
hydrofoil to Como or in the morning slip
the dinghy around the point to the lower

town or climb the hill to the castle keep.
Reg not only climbed to San Martino
but on up, then down a goat trail that sheared

the mountain's face. Charles nodded off to sleep
on the boat we took one day to Menaggio.
We all do what we think we like. The fear

of heights holds most of us to flat places:
flea markets, bocce courts, sailboat races.

7. *In the Formal Garden*

The little dog lies in the boxwood tomb
the late princess had the gardeners frame
over his grave. You can step in anytime,
sit and contemplate in the cool, clipped room

a dog's life or your own. By this green home
the small shrubs take on shapes that seem to climb
the hill. Their leafy ears and noses mime
daily unfailing greetings as they come

to cluster round His Majesty. No call
from master, mistress, or slave can sway them from
their devotion. The terrace is fresh with

roses, and if dogs have ghosts, then Wurstl
would never want to leave. I think the balm
of Gilead alone would hold me to this

garden and the Villa Serbelloni if
I were to end here, my tomb on the cliff.

8. *At the South Gate*

At the south gate you turn the lock and step out
onto the cobblestone track that leads to
Bellagio. To leave the grounds here is to
feel suddenly mortal, dead fish about

your feet where the daily wind heavy with clouds
has whipped the refuse in. Pescallo through
a thick sky threatens you with houses so new
the windows have no voice. Old homes are loud

against the rain, their roofs rust red and tile.
Back beyond the wall and up the hill, the view
is not the same. From that height Tennyson

might do an idyll. At the end of the quarter-mile
mule track from Bellagio, it's not so true
an Eden that you don't smell fish. The sun

never breaks through enough to make boat oil
on the wings of Chinese geese a rainbow royal.

9. *In Another Country*

With my hands I scoop the deep stone bowl free
of muck the trees and wind have deposited
over the years. Strange to find a Celtic
metate worn down by grinding so deep

so far above the lake and old grain fields.
A low stele of granite, a stile, a nick
in time, this bowl, this horn of plenty, has fed
the multitudes. Strange, too, to think what zeal

they must have had to bring the grain this far
for grinding. More than a simple stone, it was
a sacrament long before the Romans

came to build a tower on the hill. The dark
stone speaks of loss. In another country, I push
aside the leaves, and my own loss begins

to fade: the song I make is a poor offering
beside this stone. I should bring gold and grain.

10. *Grand Marnier*

By the sidewalk begonias of Bellagio
the village loony seems sane. *Si, limone*
he demands in a gruff dwarf's voice gone
cancerous from cigarettes and vino.

He takes chosen tourists by the arm, although
most bolt away, and with his red hat worn
sadly to the side speaks to them of his own
lost love. *Eh, voglio il mio amore!* So

insistent he is that some are drawn to hear
his tale. He prefers Grand Marnier and lemon
tarts. Tears start under the awning of cafes

much better than on the quay and the lire
are larger. The bells of San Giacomo at noon
call him to rest. With fixed eyes he sways

up the narrow alley toward the top of town
where he will sleep until need drives him down.

11. *Room with a View*

Behind us, one terrace up, a cherry tree
is heavy with fruit, just beyond our reach,
but Roberto has promised a ladder. Each
day we feast farther up the hill, the free

cherries sweeter than any fruit we see
in the markets of Bellagio. The beech
trees give us lordly shade, and cherries teach
morality: we are too greedy to be

this blessed. We spit the pits and pay no mind.
From our door we contemplate the nearer tree:
a ladder would be nice, for the cherries are

as large as plums. But Roberto cannot find
his ladder, and neither stone nor stick can we
find to bring the cherries down. It's hell, or

else we are living wrong. Not even our room
with a view can lift the need for cherries soon.

12. Rowing over the Dead

Lake Como is calm in the morning mist
that shrouds the promontory and carries
voices in from Varenna or the ferries
slipping across to invisible docks. The risk

is slight we will ship any water, the lisp
of the oars a soft comfort as we hurry
over the drowned white cliff where the harried
dead monks ride their stone ship, forever missed

by none lately come this way. Their cracked tomb
slid into the depths to make the lake safe for
weekend regattas of silk merchants from

Como and Milan. We cross shadows, numb
with thoughts of resurrection. The rocks near
us are white with the droppings of gulls come

to fish this inland glacial sea. They squawk
at us as if to mock our mawkish thoughts.

13. *Pub Hemingway*

The hydrofoil speeds us down the long lake
to Como to shop for silk at 6 via Geno.
The end of the lake is calm: there is no
tourist traffic in the early mist. The fate

of nations has hung on the courtyard gates
of kings in this town, where everyone knows
everyone's game. In war or peace heroes
have come and gone, but Como never fades,

they say. Nothing changes here except silk
prices. At the Villa Binda, we choose a shawl
and tie and pay thousands of lire for shades

of color we never thought Italian gilt
could be. We do not tour the church that calls
each hour by Lombardy name with bells and beads.

Instead, yellow neon flashing toward midday
lures us down the street to Pub Hemingway.

14. *Taking the Varenna Ferry*

After a morning's climb up the mountain
backing Varenna, we lounge on the quay
with our feet in the water. We cannot see
Castello di Vezio from here. A thin

fog hides the mountaintop where we began
to understand the trails of Lombardy
the hard way. We came early in the day
by ferry to make the climb, and now again

we are glad to take the ferry back across
to Bellagio, innocents going home,
leaving the locked tower of Vezio above

the mist. The elder ferryman signals us
on board but waves away tickets: we have gone
so often across he smiles at us with love

or the knowledge we will be crossing more
than we think to try the castello's door.

15. *La Maranese, Villa Serbelloni*

From the window of my study, I look south,
down the sloping olive orchard to the boat-
house and beyond. The lake lies like a moat
for the promontory. No one without

a proper password enters here. About
us everywhere the blackbirds sing of what
they have: what we would like to have, a lot
protected by high walls. Their trilling shouts

of destiny echo through the white rooms
of La Maranese, and I am where
I want to be, looking south toward Lecco,

remembering wrong Sfondrati and doomed
pilgrims buried in the Frati, no star
above their final dust to light a soul.

Standing here free, I feel my spirit rise:
four full weeks we will live in paradise.

Three hundred feet above the lake, the fort
is turning back from stone to soil. The high
wall crumbles daily onto the grass by
the retaining wall we sit on to court

the destiny we read on wings that sort
the wind below into messages cried
by gulls. White against the black lake they fly
infinite figure eights below the fort,

guarding their nests on the sheer cliff's face.
We hear the wind beneath and other sounds
we cannot identify. Something chthonian

is tunneling into our lives. This place
takes hold of us and draws our eyes around
precipitous ways. The risks that we take on

climbs would make a sane man dizzy. We run
the trails that lead us to more than ruins.

17. *The Paying Stone*

Many a soul shipped oars, boats bumping rock,
where Serbelloni left his jar of vinegar.
At the stone, citizens of Bellagio or
neighboring villages were required to drop

their payment in the jar. Coins only. To stop
the plague from spreading up the hill, the jar
was not to be touched at all. The archers
on the cliff would see to that, crossbows cocked

at every boat. Serbelloni behind his guarded walls
meant well and left supplies for the village at
the west gate. No plagued coin would cross his palm,

nor citizen live who did not pay the toll.
Villa gates stayed locked. Neither nuns nor rats
could breach Serbelloni's walls. Death songs and psalms

moved him to a hard provisioning: he kept
his own men busy tunneling into the depths.

18. *South Wind*

The day we row to Villa Giulia
starts clear and calm, the surface of the lake
smooth and green. Cafe terraces in the wake
of the dinghy fall away soft as villa

songs wafting out from Pescallo. No Scylla
lurks beneath and no sirens curse the lake
this early in the day, though we know a late
wind always comes up from the south, a killer

for small boats. But light turns heavy with clouds
before we reach the villa's dock, and the wind
picks up force early and makes me pull the oars

hard. The day grows dark, a nasty shroud
of rain covers us, and the lake and rain
become one mass. We are blind to the shore

we may never touch again. Nothing to do
but go with the wind that has our boat in tow.

19. *Mafia Wedding*

After the long dinner and drinks, we hear
the sound of horns and see, below, a line
of car lights moving slowly up behind
Bellagio as if all Rome were driving here.

We do not understand why the lights appear
to flash for miles. Justin suggests a crime
has been avenged or a Mafia wedding. Anne
lets us marvel at the sound of horns till tears

of laughter spill over her face. Soccer,
she says. Italy continues to win. The World
Cup is up for grabs. We remember old news,

and the romance of the night becomes locker
room gossip. Here, where day after day unfurls
for us infinite art, we usually use

our hearts to explain the night. So let it stand:
a wedding, lights the confetti and horns the band.

20. *Regatta*

Four weeks we have lived among the ghosts of gone
writers, artists, historians, scholars
of all sorts. We can hear them at the doors
of the library, the floor creaking, a blown

curtain rising from no wind where the lonely
princess died. The Villa Serbelloni flowers
bloom for all of them. In only hours
now we too will leave the beautiful lawn,

forest, cliff, and looking back will dream
only a ghost of the paradise we knew.
We will see shades of ourselves walking there,

down through the olive orchard, across the stream
the trail becomes in rain, to Pescallo to
watch the regatta set all the white sails for

Varenna, where the right wind blows. We will
remember this even though our minds grow still.

The Frati: Crypt, Chapel, Oboe

below the Villa Serbelloni
for Peter and Jean Platt

The courtyard is full of sun and weeds. Stone
gives way to grass. Silence spreads down
the colonnade as fast as shadows of clouds.
Each door is a station of the cross, although
now no brothers pray in cells, no brothers go
forth at dawn to work the villa. The drone
of traffic in Bellagio gives way to the bells
of San Giacomo down the hill. At noon the tone
is definitely Lombard, as mournful
as the plague, ringing of medieval death.
A death's-head marks the only unlocked door.
Behind it shadow is a constant shroud, the floor

dry with ash someone tried to teach a lesson
with, or to clean the stone. A dozen tombs
and just one bears an epitaph: *Pellegrino*
da Lecco in charcoal. And underneath, a skull
and crossed bones in char. Above in white quiet,
Peter Platt, full of song lines, changes a dull
reed, then strokes his oboe into music
for God, long absent from this empty house.
The chapel quivers with chords bounding off
its rejuvenated walls. The wooden mouse-
gnawed cross fills one wall, and the air is thick
with motes of paint and dry rot drifting softly

through the oboe's sacred abo songs. Peter plays
for all the walls, and the walls play back.

Peter plays, and God comes down and sits on
the front-row pew and sings a chorus, mourns
the Frati gone and even Sfondrati's lost son
who became a priest to expiate the black
sins of the father. Then God sings other
worlds equally sweet and far. Not God, but Peter's
oboe's songs, winged down under holy words
bringing into this lifted fallen house hope,
rendering through reed and simple wood a mood
such as no sermon alone could ever do.

The Monks of Villa Serbelloni

for Roberto and Gianna

The dinghy laps the waves across the black
water below the ruins no one can name
with certainty. You think of monks in sack-

cloth down in their stone ship, untouched by fame
the Villa has come to know. The gull cries break
the morning fog that rises from the same

source as perch flapping the surface of the lake
to test the light. You half expect Geryon
to rock the boat and offer you his neck.

Dead under cliff and gulls, heavily you turn
the boat toward shore, over the exact spot
the monks went down. The sun begins to burn

the fog away. The wind grows southerly, not
what you expect: it forces in odd trash
from Lecco. The time part of the cliff leaned out

into the lake, tombs towering over fish,
was a day Dante would've loved, awaiting the fall.
Or Pliny, who'd write a note to Tacitus

from Villa Tragedia. For this late burial
by water, the civil engineers went to
great expense to ensure the slab would fall,

by dynamite and civic will, into
the depths the monks sought to lie above with
ease until judgment day. Uneasy, you

cross the dark water, watching for signs of fish
you will never recall the name of, bony
beyond belief. The dull wind brings more trash

from Lecco. Call it votive offerings from Rome.
You cross the sunken stone against the wind,
rowing hard and remembering *your* brief home

nine ledges up the hill. Lombardy bells send
word all over Bellagio that your time
at the Villa Serbelloni is near an end.

Notes

Page 14ff.   Winding Stair Mountain is situated in eastern Oklahoma,
                    LeFlore County, and is a large part of the westernmost area
                    of the Ouachita National Forest.

Page 47ff.   Fourche Maline is a stream flowing eastward out of the
                    western end of the Sans Bois Mountains, Latimer County,
                    Oklahoma.

Page 55   *Mali chito* is Choctaw for *tornado,* or any big wind.

Page 56   *Achukma* is Choctaw for *peace.*

Page 92ff.   The Frati is a seventeenth-century monastery on the Villa
                    Serbelloni grounds in Bellagio, Italy.

Poetry from Illinois

History Is Your
Own Heartbeat
Michael S. Harper (1971)

The Foreclosure
Richard Emil Braun (1972)

The Scrawny Sonnets and
Other Narratives
Robert Bagg (1973)

The Creation Frame
Phyllis Thompson (1973)

To All Appearances: Poems
New and Selected
Josephine Miles (1974)

The Black Hawk Songs
Michael Borich (1975)

Nightmare Begins
Responsibility
Michael S. Harper (1975)

The Wichita Poems
Michael Van Walleghen (1975)

Images of Kin: New and
Selected Poems
Michael S. Harper (1977)

Poems of the Two Worlds
Frederick Morgan (1977)

Cumberland Station
Dave Smith (1977)

Tracking
Virginia R. Terris (1977)

Riversongs
Michael Anania (1978)

On Earth as It Is
Dan Masterson (1978)

Coming to Terms
Josephine Miles (1979)

Death Mother and Other
Poems
Frederick Morgan (1979)

Goshawk, Antelope
Dave Smith (1979)

Local Men
James Whitehead (1979)

Searching the Drowned
Man
Sydney Lea (1980)

With Akhmatova at
the Black Gates
Stephen Berg (1981)

Dream Flights
Dave Smith (1981)

More Trouble with
the Obvious
Michael Van Walleghen (1981)

The American Book of
the Dead
Jim Barnes (1982)

The Floating Candles
Sydney Lea (1982)

Northbook
Frederick Morgan (1982)

Collected Poems, 1930–83
Josephine Miles (1983)

The River Painter
Emily Grosholz (1984)

Healing Song for the Inner Ear
Michael S. Harper (1984)

The Passion of the
Right-Angled Man
T. R. Hummer (1984)

Dear John, Dear Coltrane
Michael S. Harper (1985)

Poems from the Sangamon
John Knoepfle (1985)

Eroding Witness
Nathaniel Mackey (1985)
National Poetry Series

In It
Stephen Berg (1986)

Palladium
Alice Fulton (1986)
National Poetry Series

The Ghosts of Who
We Were
Phyllis Thompson (1986)

Moon in a Mason Jar
Robert Wrigley (1986)

Lower-Class Heresy
T. R. Hummer (1987)

Poems: New and Selected
Frederick Morgan (1987)

Cities in Motion
Sylvia Moss (1987)
National Poetry Series

Furnace Harbor: A
Rhapsody of the North Country
Philip D. Church (1988)

The Hand of God and
a Few Bright Flowers
William Olsen (1988)
National Poetry Series

Bad Girl, with Hawk
Nance Van Winckel (1988)

Blue Tango
Michael Van Walleghen (1989)

The Great Bird of Love
Paul Zimmer (1989)
National Poetry Series

Eden
Dennis Schmitz (1989)

Waiting for Poppa
at the Smithtown Diner
Peter Serchuk (1990)

Great Blue
Brendan Galvin (1990)

Stubborn
Roland Flint (1990)
National Poetry Series

What My Father Believed
Robert Wrigley (1991)

Something Grazes Our Hair
S. J. Marks (1991)

The Surface
Laura Mullen (1991)
National Poetry Series

Walking the Blind Dog
G. E. Murray (1992)

The Sawdust War
Jim Barnes (1992)